Preface

The evolution of computer science has elevated algorithm design as a cornerstone of problem-solving in both academic research and industry practice. As the complexity of computational challenges continues to grow, mastering algorithmic thinking has become essential for anyone pursuing a career in technology or aiming for academic excellence. The aim of this book, Introduction to Algorithm Design: Previous Years Unsolved Papers, is to provide learners with a platform to enhance their analytical and problem-solving capabilities through a curated selection of unsolved questions from previous years' examinations.

This book emphasizes a hands-on approach, inviting readers to engage directly with intricate problems spanning core algorithmic topics such as sorting, searching, dynamic programming, graph theory, and more. By grappling with these questions, learners develop deeper insights into algorithm efficiency, optimization, and application.

We have designed this book to serve both undergraduate students seeking a deeper understanding of algorithms and professionals preparing for competitive exams or technical interviews. Each problem has been carefully selected to represent a diverse range of difficulty levels, offering a comprehensive challenge for learners at any stage.

We hope this book becomes an invaluable tool in your journey towards mastering algorithm design and encourages you to approach complex computational problems with confidence and precision.

Table of Contents

BCS – 042

Bachelor Of Computer Applications (BCA) (Revised)
Chapter 1: Term-End Examination, June,2014
BCS-042: Introduction to Algorithm Design

Time: 2 Hours
Maximum Marks: 50

Note: (i) Question No. 1 is compulsory.
(ii) Attempt any three Questions from the rest.

Section - A

1. (a) Given the following list of 8 integers, sort them using insertion sort. Determine the number of comparisons used by the sorting algorithm as well as the total number of assignment operations. 8

25	15	7	10	8	12	6	13

Show the process of sorting.
(b) Define θ(big theta) notation. By using a basic definition, show that $5n^2+9n-8=\theta(n^2)$ 4
(c) Draw all the spanning trees of the following weighted connected graph. 3

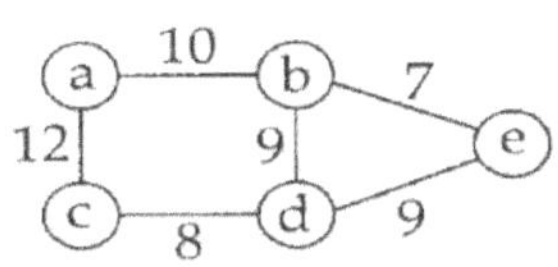

(d) What is a recurrence relation? What is an initial condition? Define recurrence relation and initial conditions for the following: 5
(i) Fibonacci sequence
(ii) Factorial function

Section - B

2. Define a fractional knapsack problem. Find the optimal solution to the following instance of a knapsack problem. Show step-by-step running of the algorithm. 10
Number of objects: n=5n
Capacity of knapsack: M=10
$(P_1,P_2,P_3,P_4,P_5) = (12, 32, 40, 30, 50)$
$(W_1,W_2,W_3,W_4,W_5) = (4, 8, 2, 6, 1)$

Where Pi is profit and
Wi - is weight.

Each object has a profit Pi and weight Wi. The problem is to fill a knapsack (up to its maximum capacity M) which maximizes the total profit earned.

3. Write Kruskal's algorithm and apply it to find a Minimum Spanning Tree (MST) of the following graph. Also, discuss the complexity of the algorithm. **10**

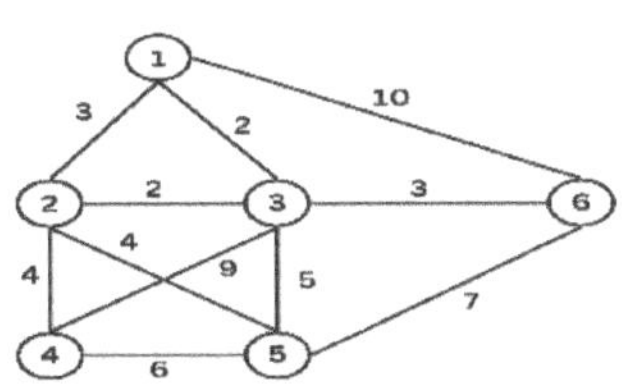

4. (a) Define the following terms: 8
(i) Mathematical Induction
(ii) Dynamic programming technique

(iii) Optimization problem
(iv) Single source shortest path problem
(b) What is a complete graph? Draw a complete graph with four vertices. **2**

5. (a) For the given graph, write DFS and BFS traversal sequence from the node A. **8**

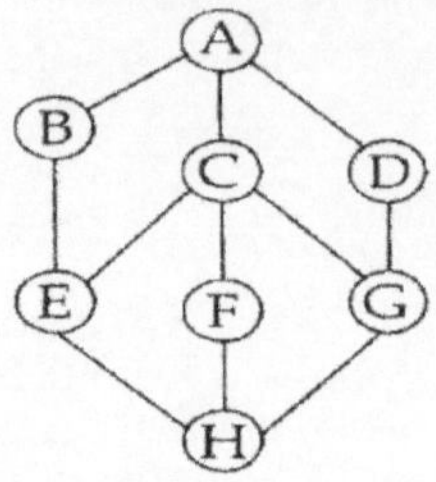

(b) Arrange the following growth rates in increasing order: 2

3O(3^n),O(n^2),O(1),O(n log n)O

BCS – 042

Bachelor Of Computer Applications (BCA) (Revised)
Chapter 2: Term-End Examination, December,2014
BCS-042: Introduction to Algorithm Design

Time: 2 Hours
Maximum Marks: 50

Note: (i) Question No. 1 is compulsory.
(ii) Attempt any three Questions from the rest.

Section A

1. (i) Given a list of integers (shown below), determine the number of comparisons and assignment operations used by bubble sort to sort the list. Show the process of sorting. **10**

35	8	7	15	25	30	10	12

Perform worst-case analysis.

(ii) Prove or disprove the following using the basic definition of O(big Oh): **2**
$5n^2+8n+15=O(n^2)$

(iii) Group the following functions by complexity category: **2**
2^n, n, n!, $\sqrt{n}$, 4n+12

(iv) Apply DFS and BFS to the complete graph on four vertices. List the vertices in the order they would be visited. **6**

SECTION B

2. Write Prim's algorithm and apply it to find the minimum cost spanning tree for the following graph: **10**

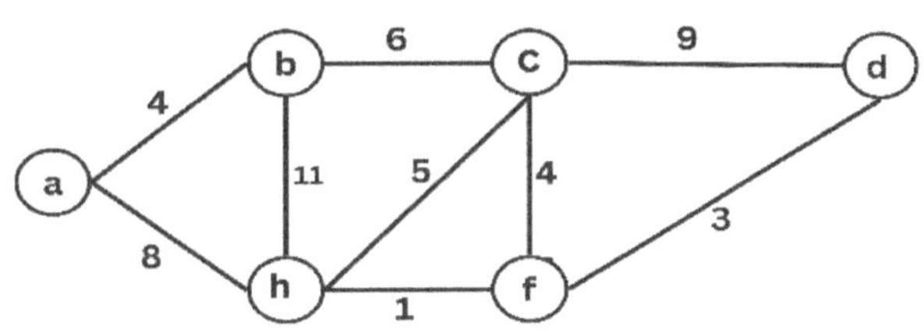

3. Illustrate the working of a binary search tree while searching for the element 14 in the following sorted array:

8	14	20	25	35	45	50	85	95	100

Also, analyze the algorithm for the best and worst cases. **10**

4. (i) What is a recurrence relation? Write a recurrence equation for any algorithm that follows the Divide and Conquer strategy and explain it. **5**
(ii) Define the following terms: **5**
Backtracking
Dynamic Programming
Time Complexity
Asymptotic Analysis
Upper Bound

5. (i) Suppose you are given currency notes of all denominations, e.g., 2, 5, 10, 15, 20, 100, 500. Further, it is assumed that currency notes of each denomination are available in sufficient numbers for the purpose of using the minimum number of notes. The problem is to find the minimum number of currency notes to make the amount of 437 using the Greedy approach. Show the sequence of steps for the selection and rejection of notes. **6**

(ii) Define the following terms: **4**
Connected Graphs
Path

Cycle
Tree

BCS – 042

Bachelor Of Computer Applications (BCA) (Revised)
Chapter 3: Term-End Examination, June, 2015
BCS-042: Introduction to Algorithm Design

Time: 2 Hours
Maximum Marks: 50

Note: (i) Question No. 1 is compulsory.
(ii) Attempt any three Questions from the rest.

1. (a) Write an algorithm to compute a^n by left-to-right binary exponentiation method and illustrate through an example. **6**

(b) Do the complexity analysis of the above algorithm. **4**

(c) Put the following classes of algorithms in increasing order of growth: **2**

$O(2^n), O(n \log_2 n), O(\log_2 n), O(n)$

(d) Using the definition of Big Oh, show that $6n^2 + 20\,n = O(n^3)$. **4**

(e) What is the difference between a graph and a tree? Draw four spanning trees of the following graph: **4**

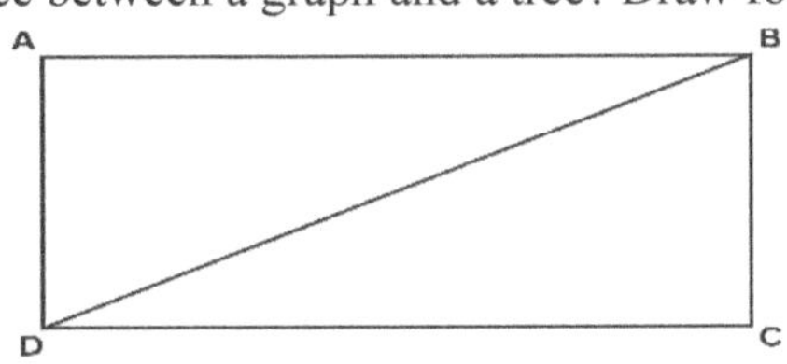

2. Apply Kruskal's algorithm to find a minimum cost spanning tree of the following graph: **10**

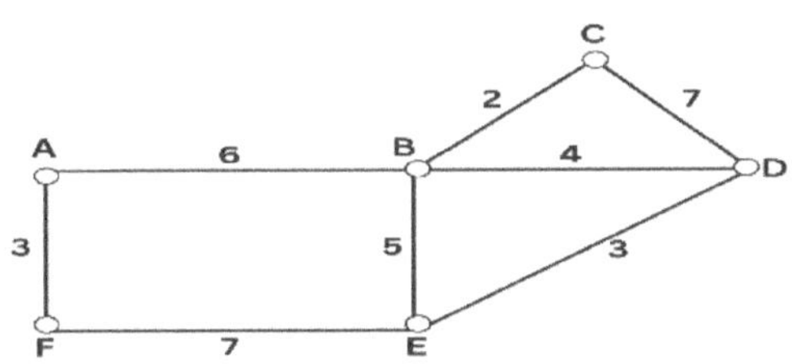

3. (a) Apply the Merge Sort algorithm to sort the following list: 6

15	5	8	7	4	20	25

(b) Describe any two methods of solving the recurrence relation. 4

4. Explain the following terms with examples: 10

(a) Complete graph
(b) Combinatorial problems
(c) Branch and bound technique
(d) Loose bound
(e) Average case

5. (a) Find the optimal solution to the knapsack instance (fractional): 6

n=5, M=10

(P1,P2,P3,P4,P5) = (14, 24, 32, 18, 20)

(W1,W2,W3,W4,W5) = (7, 8, 4, 3, 5)

(b) What is a single source shortest path problem? What are the proposed solutions? 4

BCS – 042

Bachelor Of Computer Applications (BCA) (Revised)
Chapter 4: Term-End Examination, December, 2015
BCS-042: Introduction to Algorithm Design

Time: 2 Hours
Maximum Marks: 50

Note: (i) Question No. 1 is compulsory.
(ii) Attempt any three Questions from the rest.

1. (a) Using the definition of Ω, show that $6n^2 + 20n \neq \Omega(n^3)$. **4**
(b) Given a list of n distinct integers, write an algorithm to determine the position of an integer in the list using a linear search and count the number of comparison operations required. **6**
(c) By applying the induction method, show that for all positive integers n: 6

$$1^2+2^2+\ldots+n^2 = (n(n+1)(2n+1))/6$$

(d) Illustrate the representation of the following graph through an adjacency list and adjacency matrix: **4**

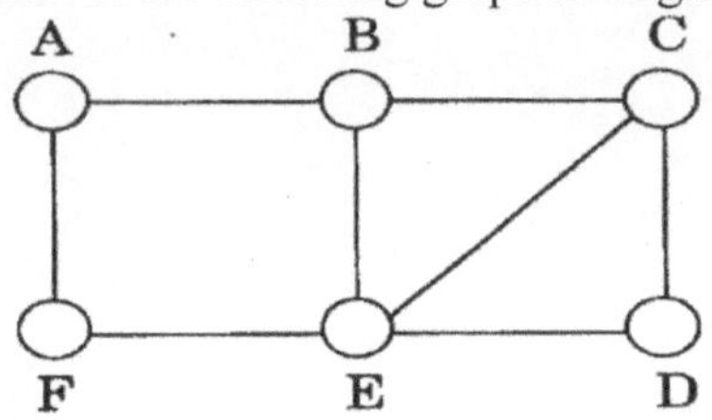

2. (a) Find the optimal solution to the knapsack (fractional) problem with n=5n = 5n=5 and m=10m = 10m=10, where n is the number of objects and mmm is the capacity of the knapsack. The profit and weight of each object are given below: **6**

$(P_1,P_2,P_3,P_4,P_5) = (10, 30, 35, 20, 40)$

$(W_1,W_2,W_3,W_4,W_5) = (3, 5, 2, 6, 1)$

(b) Write Prim's algorithm to find the minimum cost spanning tree. **4**

3. (a) Apply QuickSort to sort the following array. Show all the steps: **6**

15	5	10	8	7	2	20	30

(b) What are the worst case and best case in the QuickSort algorithm? **4**

4. Define the following terms: **10**
(a) Optimization
(b) Dynamic programming
(c) Recurrence relation
(d) Asymptotic bounds
(e) Unconnected graph

5. For the given graph, apply DFS traversal scheme and write the DFS sequence. Also, write the time complexity of DFS and BFS algorithms. **10**

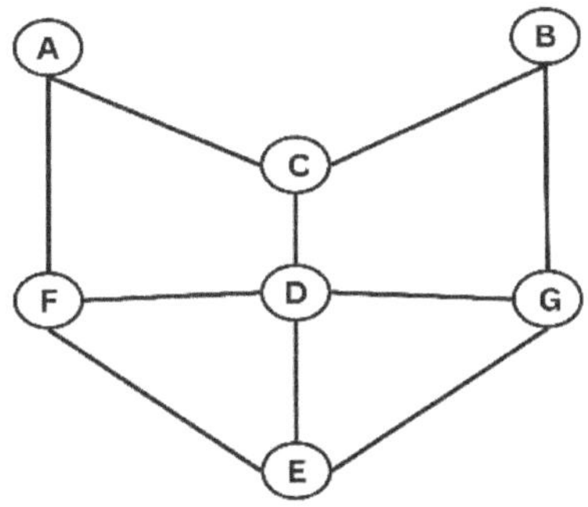
A
B
C
F
D
G
E

BCS – 042

Bachelor Of Computer Applications (BCA) (Revised)
Chapter 5: Term-End Examination, June, 2016
BCS-042: Introduction to Algorithm Design

Time: 2 Hours
Maximum Marks: 50

Note: (i) Question No. 1 is compulsory.
(ii) Attempt any three Questions from the rest.

1. (a) What is an algorithm? Briefly explain the time complexity and space complexity of an algorithm. **5**

(b) Define notation Ω (Big Omega). If $f(n)=2n^3+3n^2+1$ and $g(n)=2n^2+3$, then show $f(n)=\Omega(g(n))$. **4**

(c) Arrange the following growth rates in increasing order: **2**

$O(n^2), O(3^n), O(n), O(\log n)$

(d) Draw all minimum spanning trees of the following weighted connected graph: **4**

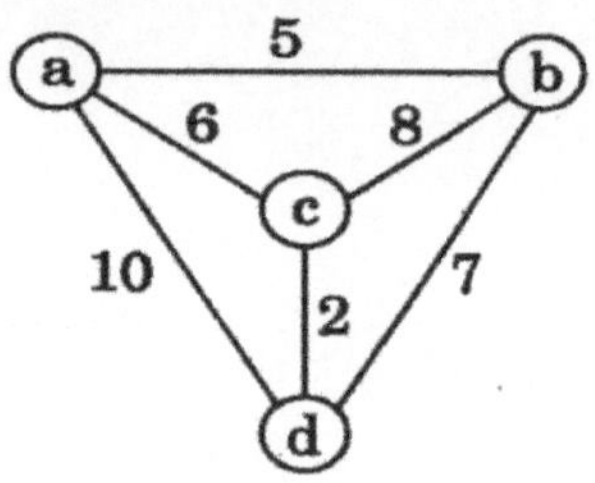

(e) Write a linear search algorithm and explain its best case, worst case, and average case time complexity. **5**

2. (a) Given the following list of 8 integers, sort them using insertion sort. Determine the number of comparisons required by the algorithm. Also, find the total number of assignment operations in this process: **8**

10	7	12	6	8	15	25	11

(b) Write any four characteristics of a greedy algorithm. **2**

3. (a) What is a recurrence relation? Draw a recursion tree for the recurrence $T(n)=2T(n-1)+1$. **4**

(b) Write the adjacency list and adjacency matrix representation of the following graph: **6**

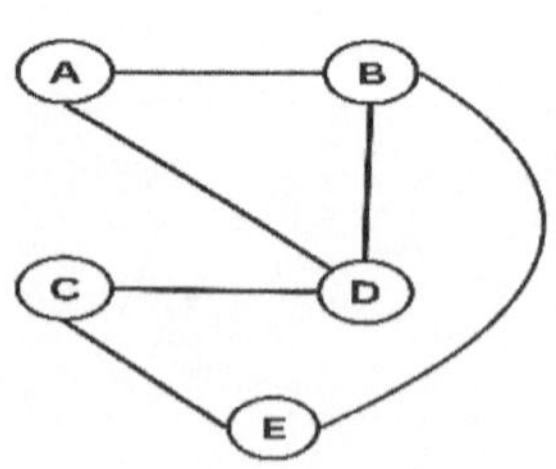

4. (a) Write a binary search algorithm and search for the value 28 in the following list using the binary search algorithm. Show the steps: **5**

1, 7, 18, 27, 28, 30, 39

(b) Write Prim's algorithm for finding the minimum spanning tree. Find the complexity of this algorithm. **5**

5. (a) Define the following terms: **4**
(i) Connected graph
(ii) Cycle in an undirected graph

(b) Consider the following fractional knapsack problem: **6**
M=20
Profits (P1,P2,P3) = (24, 24, 15)
(W1,W2,W3) = (18, 15, 10)
Show the running of the greedy algorithm for the fractional knapsack problem.

BCS – 042

Bachelor Of Computer Applications (BCA) (Revised)
Chapter 6: Term-End Examination, December,2016
BCS-042: Introduction to Algorithm Design

Time: 2 Hours
Maximum Marks: 50

Note: (i) Question No. 1 is compulsory.
(ii) Attempt any three Questions from the rest.

1. (a) Define OOO (Big Oh) notation and prove or disprove the following using the basic definition of O (Big Oh):
$2n^3+n^2+10=O(n^3)$ **4**
(b) Order the following functions in increasing order of O( ) notation: **3**
3^n, n, n!, n^2+5, $2n^2+3$, 5n+2
(c) Traverse the following graph using Depth First Search (DFS), starting from node A. **5**

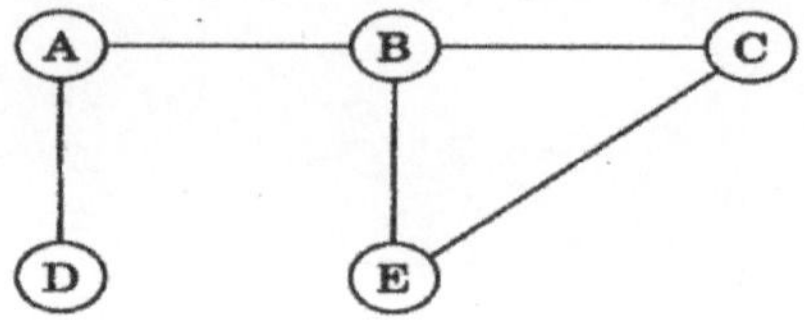

(d) Write Prim's algorithm and apply it to find the minimum cost spanning tree for the following graph: **8**

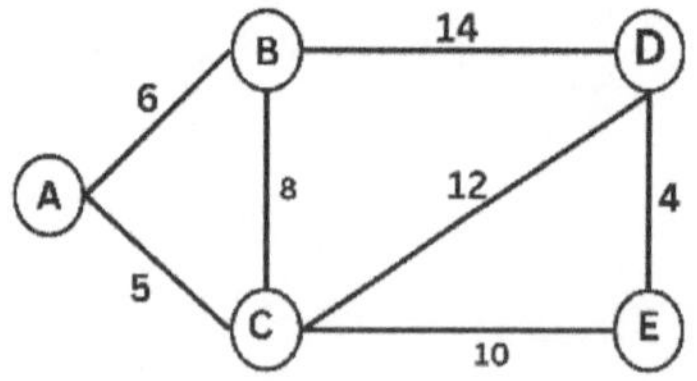

2. (a) What is a recurrence relation? Define the Fibonacci sequence using a recurrence relation. **4**
(b) Write the bubble sort algorithm and find its time complexity. **6**

3. (a) Suppose you are given scoring shots (0, 1, 2, 3, 4, 5, 6); a cricket batsman can score on one shot. Further, it is assumed that there is no limit to the number of times a batsman can score on any shot. The problem is to find the minimum number of shots required to score 100 runs using the Greedy approach. Show the sequence of steps for the selection and rejection of shots. **8**
(b) Explain the best case and worst case in the linear search algorithm. **2**
4. (a) Define the following terms in an undirected graph, where V is the set of vertices and E is the set of edges: **4**
(i) Path
(ii) Cycle
(iii) Tree
(iv) Spanning Tree
(b) Sort the following list using the Quick-Sort algorithm. Show the intermediate steps in the process: **6**

2	8	7	3	5	6	4

5. (a) Define the following terms: **6**
(i) Asymptotic lower bound of a function
(ii) Space complexity
(iii) Asymptotic upper bound of a function

(b) Write the general form of a recurrence relation for a divide-and-conquer algorithm and explain the different parts of this recurrence relation. **4**

Bachelor Of Computer Applications (BCA) (Revised)
Chapter 7: Term-End Examination, June, 2017
BCS-042: Introduction to Algorithm Design

Time: 2 Hours
Maximum Marks: 50

Note: (i) Question No. 1 is compulsory.
(ii) Attempt any three Questions from the rest.

1. (a) Write the linear search algorithm and analyze its time complexity in the worst case. 4

(b) Arrange the following functions in increasing growth order: 2

(i)O(n^3)
(ii)O(2^n)
(iii)O(log n)
(iv)O(n)

(c) Write the recursive algorithm to calculate x^n using Divide and Conquer. 4

(d) What is Minimum Cost Spanning Tree (MCST)? Apply Prim's algorithm to find MCST for the following graph: 4

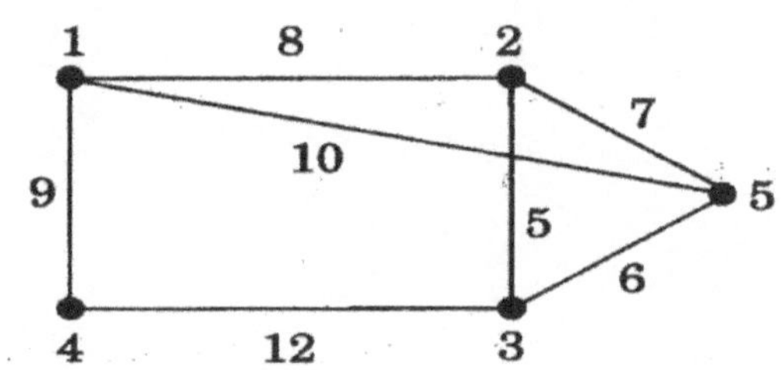

(e) Show that the worst-case time complexity of Quick sort is O(n^2), where nnn is the size of array elements. 3

(f) Create an adjacency list for the following graph: 3

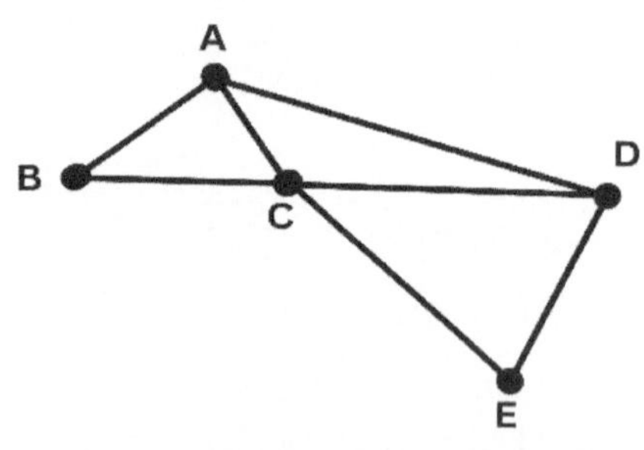

2. (a) Apply Dijkstra's algorithm to find the single-source shortest path for the following graph: 5

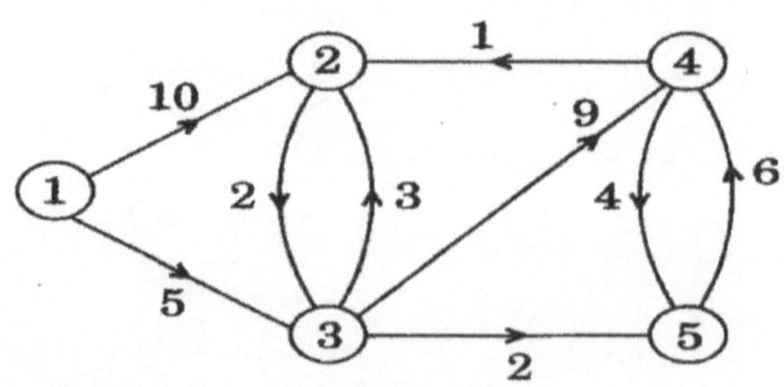

(b) Apply the Merge sort algorithm to sort the following list: 5

15, 8, 6, 12, 20, 7, 18, 5

3. (a) What is a recurrence relation? Draw a recurrence tree for the recurrence T(n) = 3T (n/2) + n 5

(b) Write the Breadth-First Search algorithm and calculate its time complexity. **5**

4. (a) Find the time complexity of the following code: **5**

```
for (i = 1; i <= n; i++)
{
  if (A[i] > B[i])
    print A[i];
}
```

(b) Find the optimal solution to the fractional knapsack problem for n=5, M (capacity of knapsack) = 10 and

$(P_1,P_2,P_3,P_4,P_5) = (12, 32, 40, 30,50)$

$(W_1,W_2,W_3,W_4,W_5) = (4, 8, 2, 6, 1)$

5. Explain the following terms with examples: **10**

(a) Space Complexity
(b) Asymptotic Notation
(c) Binary Search
(d) Master Method for Solving Recurrence

BCS – 042

Bachelor Of Computer Applications (BCA) (Revised)
Chapter 8: Term-End Examination, December, 2017
BCS-042: Introduction to Algorithm Design

Time: 2 Hours
Maximum Marks: 50

Note: (i) Question No. 1 is compulsory.
(ii) Attempt any three Questions from the rest.

1. (a) Arrange the following functions in increasing order of growth rates: **4**
(i)O(logn)
(ii)$O(n^3)$
(iii)$O(5^n)$
(iv)O(nlogn)
(b) What is an Algorithm? Briefly explain the meaning of complexity of an algorithm. **5**
(c) Define O (Big Oh) notation. Prove or disprove the following: **5**
$2n^2+3n+1=O(n^2)$
(d) Write a binary search algorithm and analyze its time complexity in the best case and in the worst case. **5**
(e) Create an adjacency matrix for the following graph: **4**

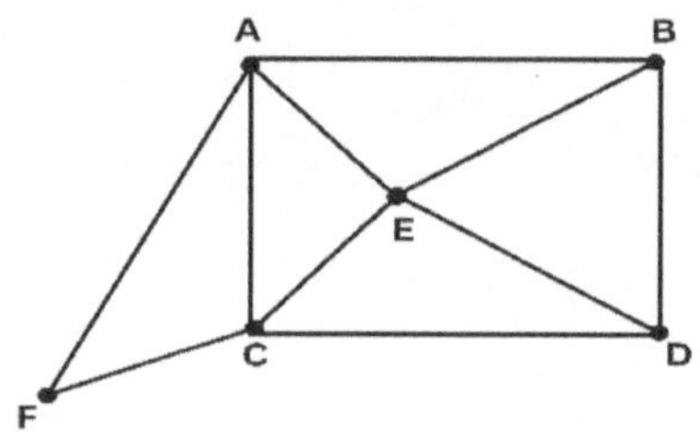

2. (a) Write an algorithm for Depth-First Search (DFS) and traverse the following graph using DFS: (Starting vertex is A) 7

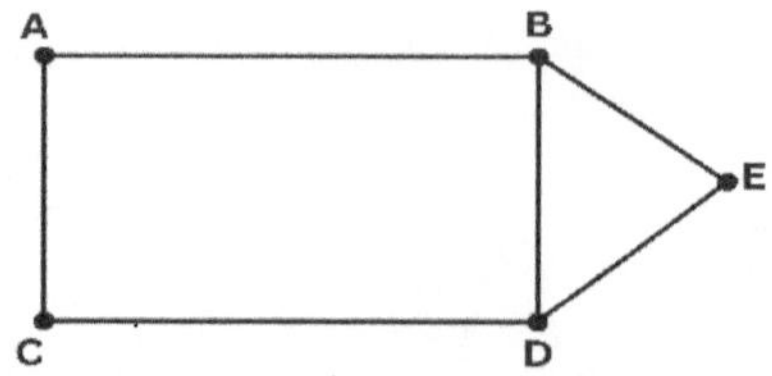

(b) Explain the difference between directed and undirected graphs. **3**

3. (a) Apply the Quick-sort algorithm to sort the following list: **5**
5, 9, 8, 4, 2, 15, 6
(b) Find the minimum cost spanning tree from the following graph using Kruskal's algorithm: **5**

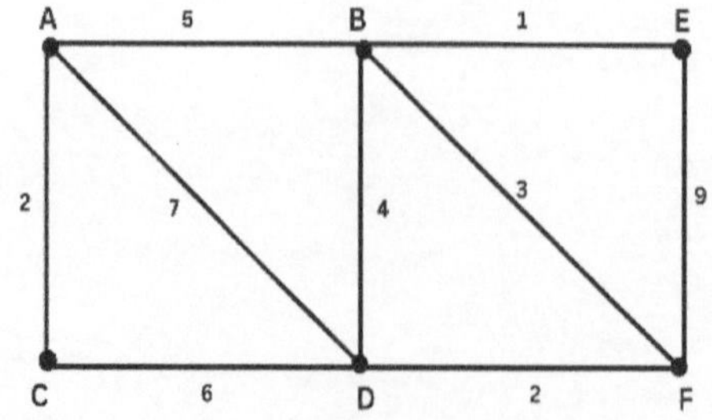

4. (a) By using mathematical induction, prove that **5**
$p(n)=1^2+2^2+3^2+\ldots+n^2=(n(n+1)(2n+1))/6$

(b) Consider the following fractional Knapsack problem: **5**
M=15 and

$$(P_1, P_2, P_3) = (25, 24, 15)$$

$$(W_1, W_2, W_3) = (18, 15, 10)$$

Show the running of the greedy algorithm for the fractional Knapsack problem.

5. Explain the following terms with examples: **10**
(a) Combinatorial Problem
(b) Complete Graph
(c) Backtracking
(d) Asymptotic Notations

BCS – 042

Bachelor Of Computer Applications (BCA) (Revised)
Chapter 9: Term-End Examination, June, 2018
BCS-042: Introduction to Algorithm Design

Time: 2 Hours
Maximum Marks: 50

Note: (i) Question No. 1 is compulsory.
(ii) Attempt any three Questions from the rest.

1. (a) Define O (Big-"Oh") notation. By using the basic definition of O, show that $3x^2+4x+1=O(x^2)$. **4**

(b) The recurrence relation for the Fibonacci sequence is given by $tn=t_{n-1}+t_{n-2}$, such that $t_0=0$ and $t_1=1$. Find the solution to this recurrence. **4**

(c) Find the optimal solution to the fractional knapsack instance n=5n = 5n=5, capacity (M)=10(M) = 10(M)=10:

P1,P2,…,P5) = (12, 32, 40, 30, 50)

(W1,W2,…,W5) = (4, 8, 2, 6, 1)

(d) Write the adjacency list and adjacency matrix representation for the following graph: **4**

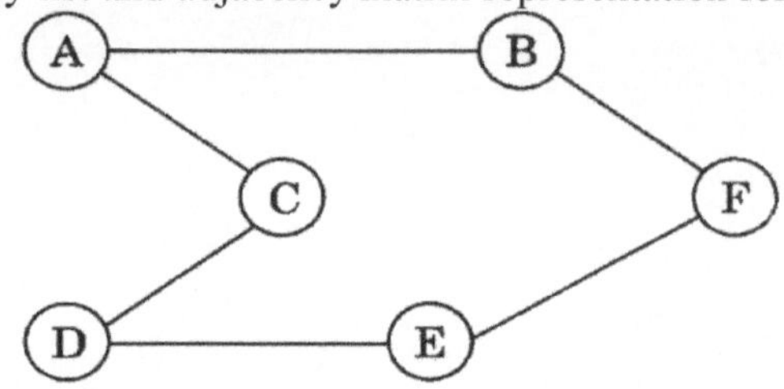

(e) Find the time complexity of the following code: **3**

```
for (i = 1; i <= n; i++)
for (j = 1; j <= n; j = j * 2)
Sum[i] = Sum[i] + i * j.
```

2. (a) Differentiate between Depth-First Search (DFS) and Breadth-First Search (BFS) in terms of time and space complexity. Traverse the following graph using: **5**
(i) DFS,
(ii) BFS, starting from node A.

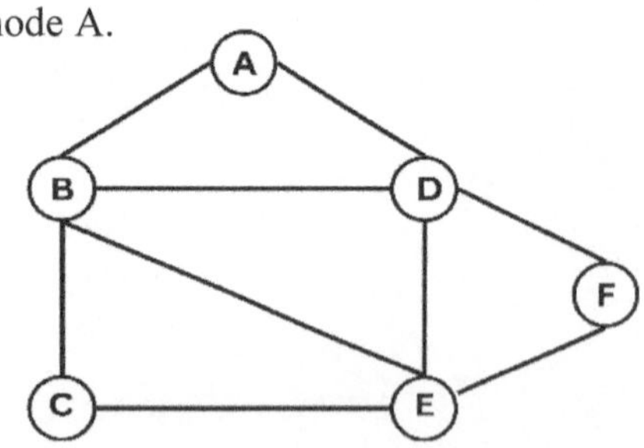

(b) List all the steps to be used to search 30 in the following list using binary search: **5**

6 8 10 12 30 32 35

3. (a) Write the Quick-sort algorithm and find its time complexity in the worst case. **5**
(b) Multiply 10265×2573 using the Divide and Conquer technique. Apply the Karatsuba method. **5**

4. (a) Write any two applications of a spanning tree. Write Prim's algorithm and apply it to find the minimum cost spanning tree for the following graph. **10**

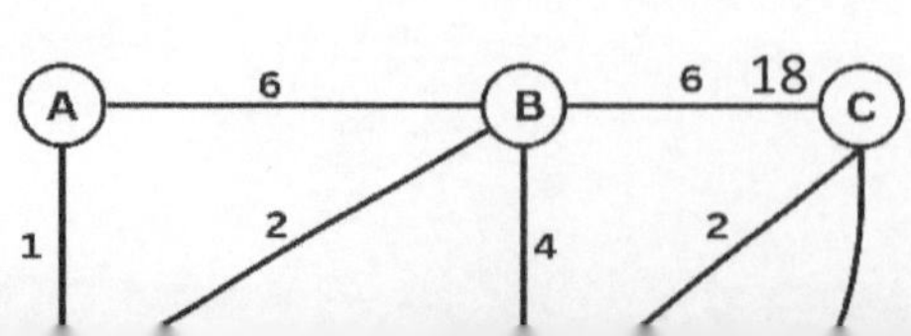

5. (a) Write all the (3) cases of the Master method for solving Recurrence. Apply the Master method to solve the following recurrence: **5**

$$T(n) = 3T(n/4) + n \log n$$

(b) Write the algorithm for bubble sort. **4**

BCS – 042

Bachelor Of Computer Applications (BCA) (Revised)
Chapter 10: Term-End Examination, December, 2018
BCS-042: Introduction to Algorithm Design

Time: 2 Hours
Maximum Marks: 50

Note: (i) Question No. 1 is compulsory.
(ii) Attempt any three Questions from the rest.

1. (a) Define Ω (Big 'Omega') notation. By using the basic definition of Ω, show that **4**
$f(n)=\Omega(g(n))$,
where $f(n)=2n^3-3n^2+1$ and
$g(n)=2n^2+3$.

(b) What is an algorithm? Explain the meaning of time complexity and space complexity of an algorithm. **6**

(c) Arrange the following functions in increasing order of growth: **3**
$n^3, 2n^2+3, 5n+2, 5^n, 2^n$

(d) Define the following terms: **4**
(i) Spanning tree
(ii) Adjacency matrix

(e) Find the time complexity of the following loop: **3**

```
for (i = 1; i <= n; i++)
{
    i = i * 2;
}
```

2. (a) Write an algorithm to multiply two square matrices of order n×n and find its time complexity. **5**

(b) Using Insertion sort, sort the following list and show all the intermediate steps: **5**
8 6 4 15 9 25 2

3. (a) Find the optimal solution to the knapsack instance n=5, capacity M=15, **7**
$(P_1,P_2,P_3,P_4,P_5) = (15, 35, 48, 30, 40)$
$(W_1,W_2,W_3,W_4,W_5) = (4, 8, 5, 6, 2)$

(b) Prove that **3**
$P(n): 1^2+2^2+\ldots+n^2=(n(n+1)(2n+1))/6$
by using mathematical induction.

4. (a) Write pseudo code for Breadth-First Search (BFS). Traverse the following graph using BFS, starting from node A. **7**

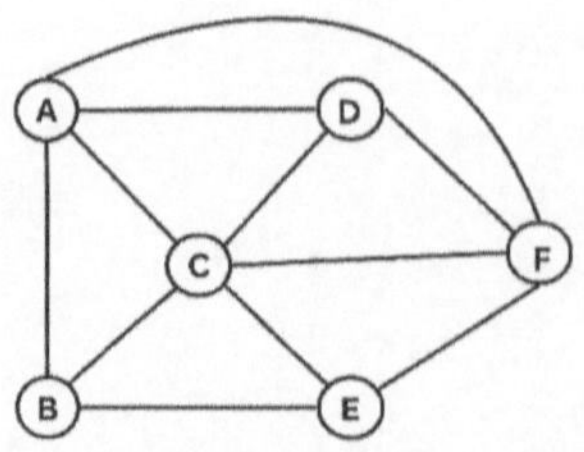

(b) Solve the following recurrence relation using the recursion tree method: **3**

T(n)=4T(n/2)+n

5. (a) Write Kruskal's Algorithm to find the Minimum Cost Spanning Tree (MCST) of the following graph: **6**

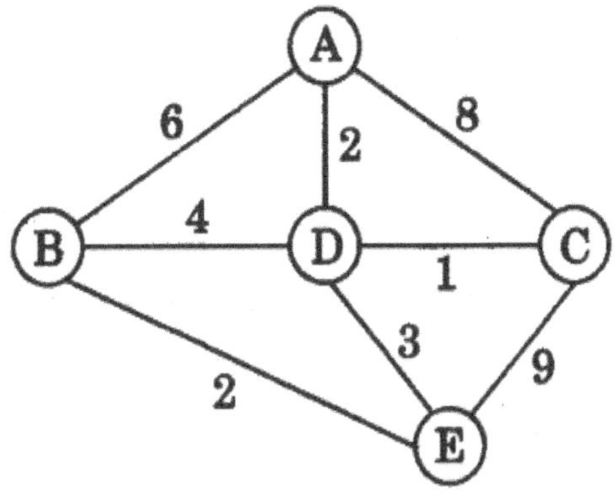

(b) Write an algorithm to search an element (say x) using Binary Search. Analyze its time complexity in the worst case. **4**

Bachelor Of Computer Applications (BCA) (Revised)
Chapter 11: Term-End Examination, June, 2019
BCS-042: Introduction to Algorithm Design

Time: 2 Hours
Maximum Marks: 50

Note: (i) Question No. 1 is compulsory.
(ii) Attempt any three Questions from the rest.

1. (a) Arrange the following functions in increasing growth order: **2**
(i)$O(n^2)$
(ii)$O(\log n)$
(iii)$O(2^n)$
(iv)$O(n\log n)$

(b) Define Θ(Theta) Notation. Let f(n) and g(n) be two positive functions. Prove or disprove the following:
(i)$f(n)+g(n)=\Theta(\min\{f(n),g(n)\})$
(ii)$3n^2+5=\Theta(n^2)$ **5**
(c) Write Prim's Algorithm to solve the Minimum Cost Spanning Tree (MCST) problem. Analyze the time complexity of the algorithm also. Apply Prim's Algorithm to the following graph and find the Minimum Cost of the Spanning Tree. (Starting Vertex 'A') **7**

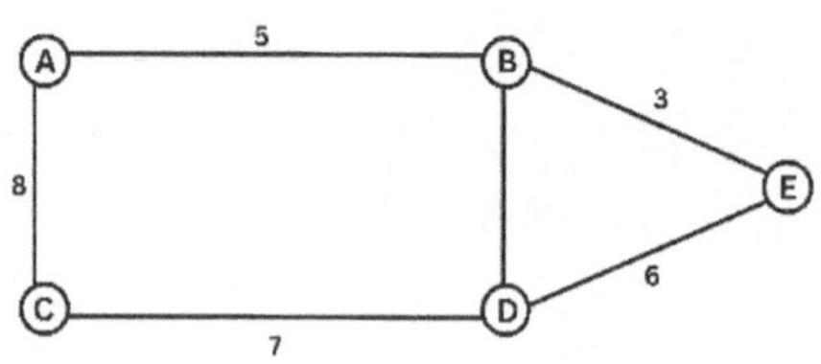

(d) Apply Recursion Tree Method to find the asymptotic upper bound for the following Recurrence:
$T(n)=2T(n/2)+n$ **4**

(e) Create an adjacency list for the following graph: **2**

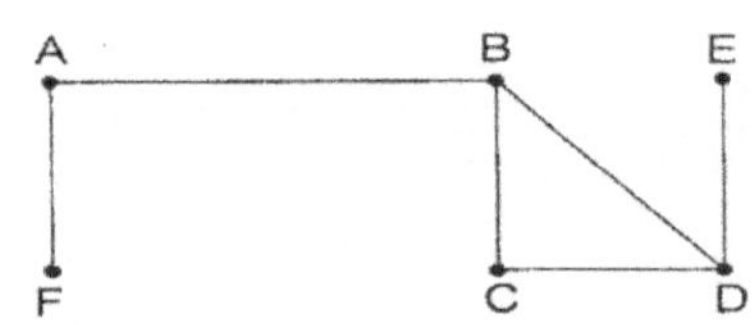

2. (a) Find the optimal solution to the Knapsack (fractional) problem where x=5 and M=10, where x is the number of objects and M is the capacity of the Knapsack. The profit and weight of each object are given below: **6**
(P1,P2,P3,P4,P5) = (10, 30, 35, 20, 40)
(W1,W2,W3,W4,W5) = (3, 5, 2, 6, 1)

(b) Multiply 2432×5219 using the Divide and Conquer Method (use the Karatsuba Method). **4**

3. (a) Apply the PARTITION procedure of QUICKSORT to the following array to find the final position of the last element (Pivot element). Show all the intermediate steps: **5**

10	15	7	6	20	9

(b) Write the DFS algorithm and find its time complexity. **5**

4. (a) Find the complexity of the following code: **3**

```
for (i = 1; i <= n; i++)
{
  for (j = 1; j <= n; j++)
  {
      if (A[j] > B[i])
        print A[j];
  }
}
```

(b) Explain the concept of RELAXING an edge in Dijkstra's Algorithm. Apply Dijkstra's Algorithm to find the shortest path for the following graph (Starting Vertex is 'A'). **7**

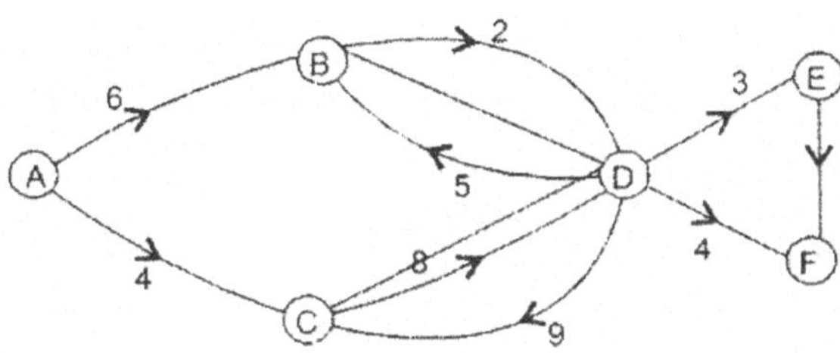

5. (a) Write an algorithm to search an element (say x) using Binary Search. Analyze the time complexity of the algorithm in the Worst Case. **5**

(b) Discuss all the three cases of the Master Method to solve the Recurrence $T(n) = aT(n/b)+f(n)$ where $a>1$, $b>1$. **5**

Bachelor Of Computer Applications (BCA) (Revised)
Chapter 12: Term-End Examination, December, 2019
BCS-042: Introduction to Algorithm Design

Time: 2 Hours
Maximum Marks: 50

Note: (i) Question No. 1 is compulsory.
(ii) Attempt any three Questions from the rest.

1. (a) Let f(n) and g(n) be two positive functions. Using the basic definition of Big Oh ("O") and Theta (Θ), prove or disprove the following: **5**

(i)$\max\{f(n),g(n)\}=O(f(n)+g(n))$
(ii)$2^n = O(2^{n+1})$

(b) Solve the following Recurrence using the Recursion tree method: **5**

$T(n) = 2T(n-1) + 1$

Find the tight solution of the Recurrence.

(c) Explain the general algorithm to solve any problem using Greedy techniques. Write any two characteristics of the Greedy Algorithm. **5**

(d) Write an algorithm to solve the Knapsack (fractional) problem using the Greedy Method. Find the running time of the algorithm also. **5**

2. (a) Define the minimum spanning tree. Apply Kruskal's Algorithm to find the minimum cost spanning tree for the following graph: **6**

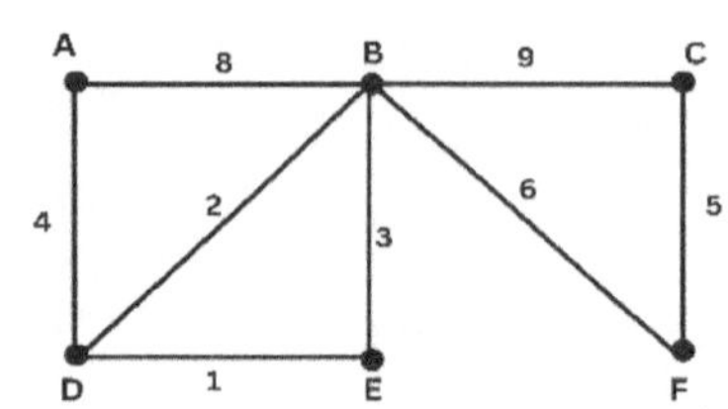

(b) Write the bubble sort algorithm and find its time complexity in the worst case. **4**

3. (a) For the following graph, write the DFS (sequence of traversal) from the node A: **4**

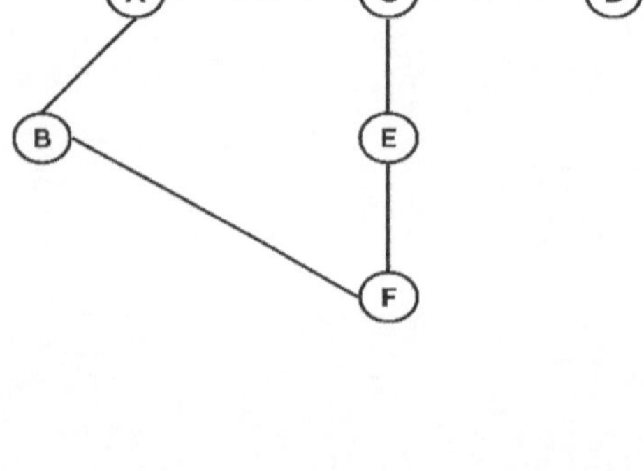

(b) Apply the Master method to solve the following recurrence relations: **6**

(i)$T(n) = 2T(n/2) + n$
(ii)$T(n) = 3T(n/4)+n \log n$

4. Explain Dijkstra's Algorithm to find a single-source shortest path in a given graph. Apply Dijkstra's Algorithm and find the shortest path from source vertex 'A' to the rest of the vertices: **10**

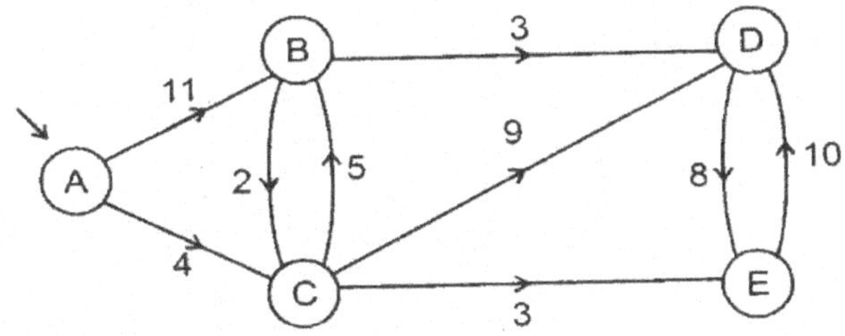

5. Differentiate between the following with respect to method of solving a problem and time complexity: **10**

(a) Depth-First Search (DFS) vs. Breadth-First Search (BFS)

(b) Bellman-Ford Algorithm vs. Dijkstra's Algorithm for a single-source shortest path.

BCS – 042

Bachelor Of Computer Applications (BCA) (Revised)
Chapter 13: Term-End Examination, June, 2020
BCS-042: Introduction to Algorithm Design

Time: 2 Hours
Maximum Marks: 50

Note: (i) Question No. 1 is compulsory.
(ii) Attempt any three Questions from the rest.

1. (a) For the function defined by: **4**
$f(n) = 5n^3+6n^2+7n+8$; show that:
(i) $f(n)=O(n^3)$
(ii) $f(n)\neq O(n)$

(b) Write an algorithm to search for the smallest number in a given array. Also, calculate its time complexity. **6**

(c) Draw all the spanning trees for the following weighted graph: **5**

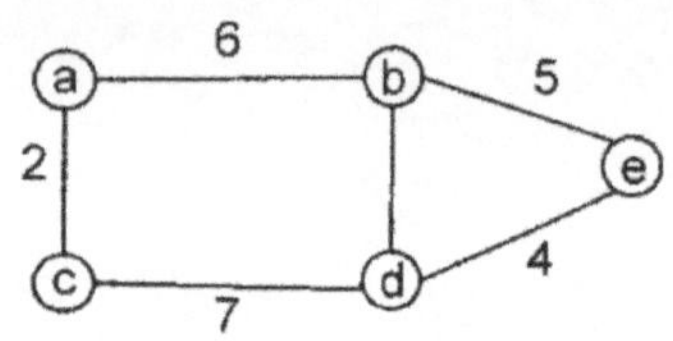

(d) For the given graph, write the DFS traversal sequence from node A: **5**

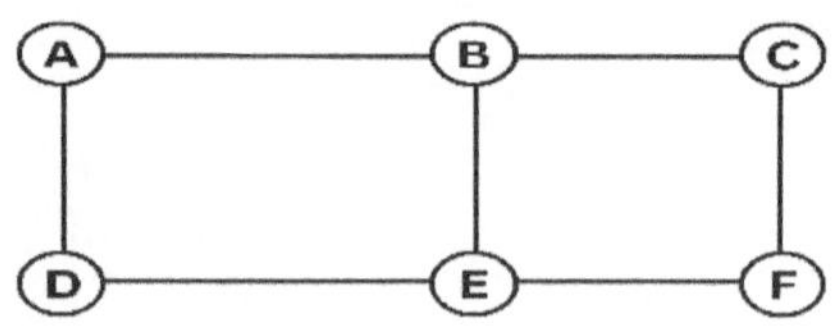

2. (a) Sort the following list of elements using Quick Sort. Also, show the intermediate steps of the operation:
29, 6, 27, 8, 6, 2, 45, 90 **6**

(b) Define an optimization problem. Give any two examples of optimization problems with explanations. **4**

3. (a) Find the optimal solution to the following fractional Knapsack problem using the Greedy Technique: **7**
(i) No. of objects n=6
(ii) Max. weight M=25
(iii) Value of each item =
$(P_1,P_2,P_3,P_4,P_5,P_6) = (10, 20, 30, 35, 45, 55)$
iv) Weight of each item =
$(W_1,W_2,W_3,W_4,W_5,W_6) = (5, 10, 12, 13, 15, 20)$

(b) Write the recurrence relation for the binary search algorithm. **3**

4. (a) Solve the following recurrence relation: **3**
$T(n)=3T(n/2) + n$

(b) Find the minimum cost spanning tree for the following graph using Kruskal's algorithm: **7**

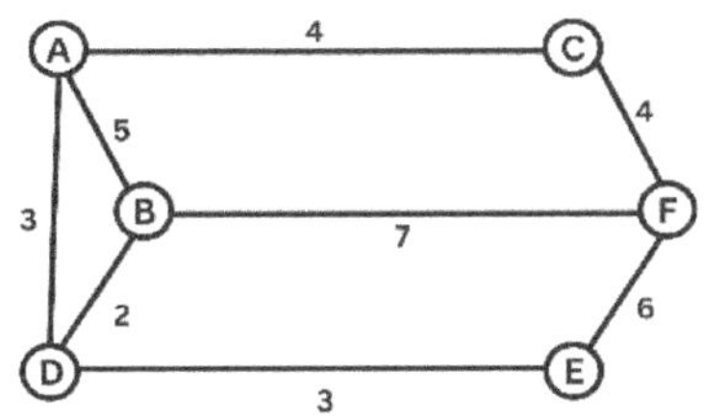

5. (a) Find the Adjacency Matrix for the following graph: **3**

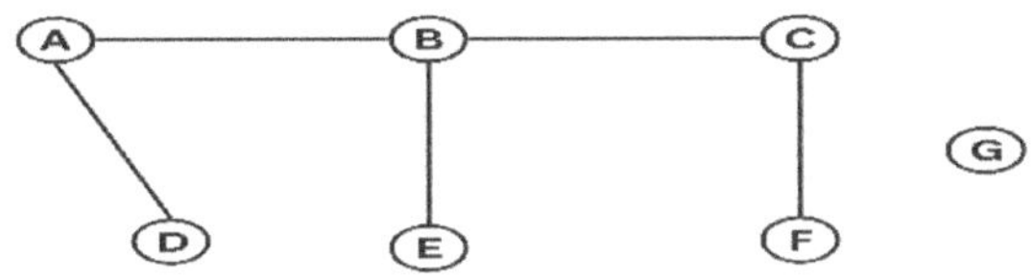

(b) Find the complexity of the following code: **4**

```
int P = 100;
while (P)
{
   for (i = 1; i <= 10; i++)
      SUM[i] = P - 1;
   P = P - 1;
}
```

Make necessary assumptions required.

(c) Describe any two methods to solve recurrence relations. **3**

Bachelor Of Computer Applications (BCA) (Revised)
Chapter 14: Term-End Examination, December, 2020
BCS-042: Introduction to Algorithm Design

Time: 2 Hours
Maximum Marks: 50

Note: (i) Question No. 1 is compulsory.
(ii) Attempt any three Questions from the rest.

1. (a) Arrange the following growth rates in increasing order of running time: **2**

$O(3^n)$, $O(n^3)$, $O(n)$, $n!$, $\log^n$

(b) Define recurrence relation and initial condition for the merge sort algorithm and explain. **4**

(c) Where is Ω\OmegaΩ (omega) notation used? For the function defined by: **4**

$f(n) = 5n^3 + 5n^2 + 1$
and $g(n)=5n^2+5$
show that:
$f(n) = \Omega(g(n)$

(d) Traverse the following graph using DFS, taking A as the starting vertex, and write the sequence of vertices in the order of their discovery. **3**

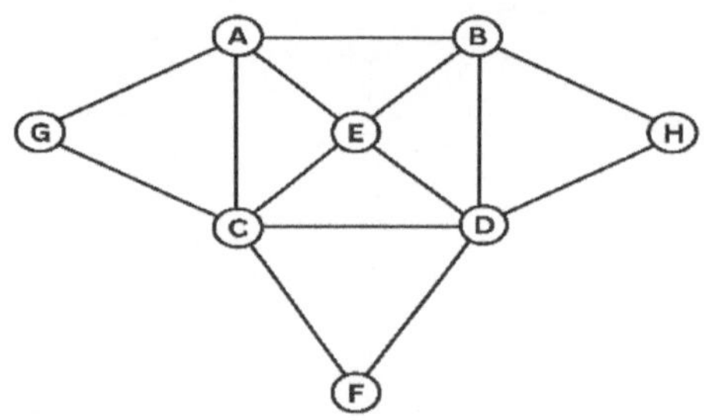

(e)(i) Apply the linear search algorithm to search for the number 4 in the following list of integer numbers. Show the starting three steps: **3**

5 15 8 4 25 30 17 20

(ii) Analyze the worst-case complexity of the above algorithm. **4**

2. (a) Find the node degree of all nodes in the graph from Q. 1 (d). **3**

(b) Write the Bellman-Ford algorithm and apply it to find the shortest path from a source vertex A to all the remaining vertices of the following directed graph. Show all the intermediate steps. **7**

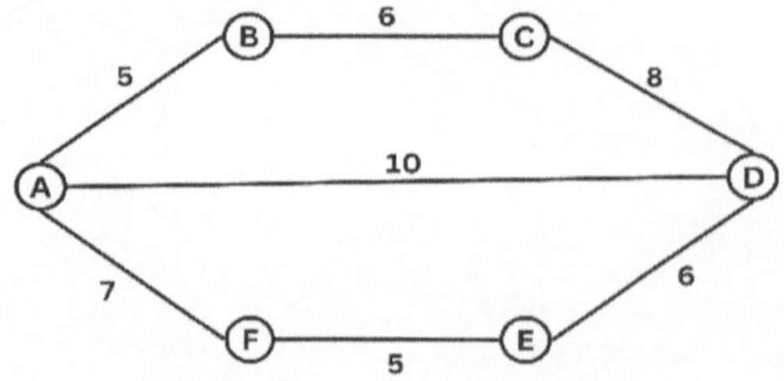

3. (a) For the two values of n=1,4, calculate the corresponding values of $n\log_2 n$. **2**

(b) Define a fractional knapsack problem. Find the optimal solution to the following instance of a knapsack problem. Show the stepwise running of the algorithm for the following example: **8**

Number of objects n=5, M=13

Capacity of a knapsack:

$(P_1, P_2, P_3, P_4, P_5) = (12, 32, 40, 30, 50)$

$(W_1, W_2, W_3, W_4, W_5) = (4, 8, 2, 6, 1)$

Where Pi is a profit and
Wi is a weight.

Each object has a profit Pi and weight Wi.

4. (a) Apply the binary search algorithm to search for a key value = 23 in the following list: **5**

6 9 13 15 23 27 35 45

(b) Perform the worst-case analysis of the above algorithm and specify an example in which the worst case will occur. **5**

5. (a) Apply Karatsuba's method to multiply 2376201 and 219237 using the divide and conquer technique. **5**

(b) Define mathematical induction. Prove the following proposition using induction: **5**

$$1^2+2^2+3^2+\ldots+n^2 = (n(n+1)(2n+1))/6$$

Bachelor Of Computer Applications (BCA) (Revised)
Chapter 15: Term-End Examination, June, 2021
BCS-042: Introduction to Algorithm Design

Time: 2 Hours
Maximum Marks: 50

Note: (i) Question No. 1 is compulsory.
(ii) Attempt any three Questions from the rest.

1. (a) Arrange the following classes of algorithms in increasing order of growth: **3**
(i)$O(n^3)$
(ii)$O(n \log n)$
(iii)$O(n^2)$
(iv)$O(\sqrt{n})$

(b) Write the recurrence relation for the following recursive function: **5**

```
int Fib(int n)
{
    if (n == 0) return 0;
if (n == 1) return 1;
else
return (Fib(n - 1) + Fib(n - 2));
}
```

(c) Sort the following list of elements using 'Insertion Sort'. Also, show intermediate steps: **6**
28, 6, 29, 90, 5, 42, 80

(d) Write the recurrence relation for the best case of the Quicksort algorithm and solve it using the Master method. **6**

2. (a) Write the pseudocode for computing GCD(m,n)GCD(m, n)GCD(m,n) and find its time complexity. **4**

(b) Write the pseudocode for Breadth First Search (BFS) and traverse the following graph using BFS starting from node A. **6**

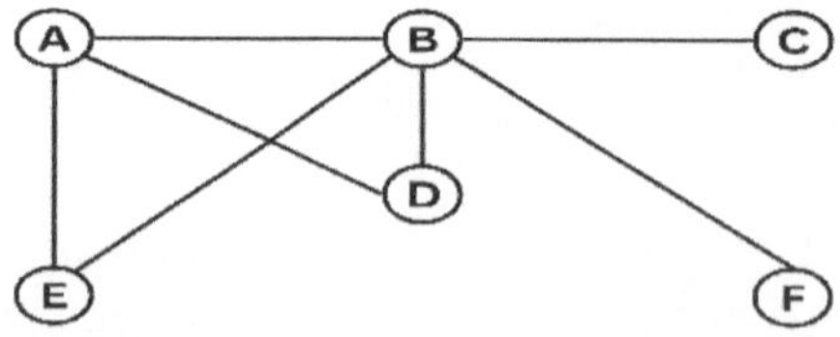

3. (a) What is the Greedy Technique? Explain the types of problems solved by using this technique. **4**

(b) Find the adjacency list for the following graph: **3**

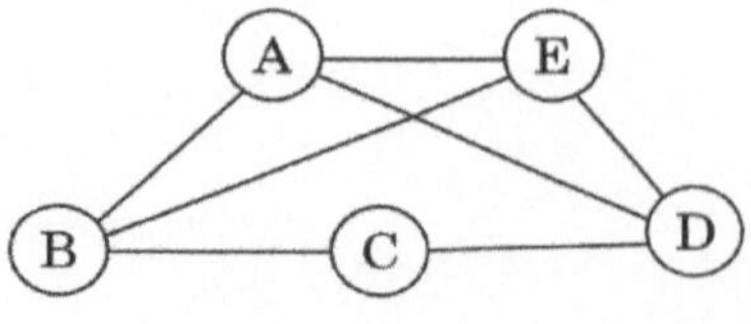

(c) With the help of an example, explain the 'Merge-Sort' technique. **3**

4. (a) What is a single source shortest path problem? Briefly explain the generic algorithm for solving it. **5**

(b) Explain the following terms with an example for each: **5**

(i) Complete Graph

(ii) Dynamic Programming Technique

5. (a) Find the minimum cost spanning tree for the following graph using Kruskal's algorithm: **7**

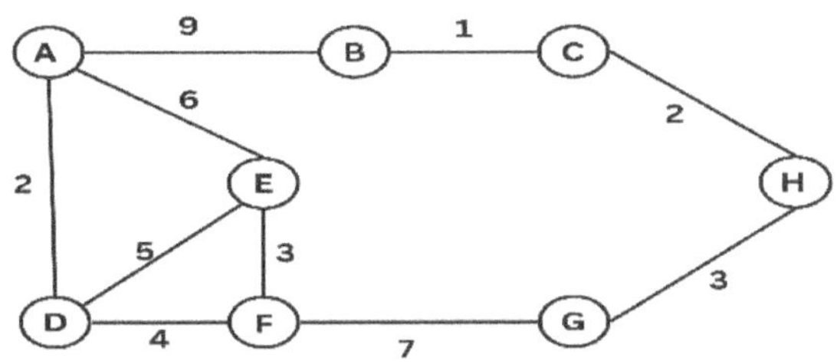

(b) Define Recurrence Relation and Initial Condition for the Factorial Function. **3**

BCS – 042

Bachelor Of Computer Applications (BCA) (Revised)
Chapter 16: Term-End Examination, December, 2021
BCS-042: Introduction to Algorithm Design

Time: 2 Hours
Maximum Marks: 50

Note: (i) Question No. 1 is compulsory.
(ii) Attempt any three Questions from the rest.

1. (a) State True or False:
$O(n \log_2 n)$ is better than $O(n^2)$ but not as good as $O(n)$. **2**

(b) Write the names of the following symbols: **2**

$\theta, \Omega, \forall, \in$

(c) Define O (Big Oh) notation. By using the basic definition of O (Big Oh), show that:
6x2+6x+1=O(x2) **4**

(d) Create an adjacency matrix for the following graph: **3**

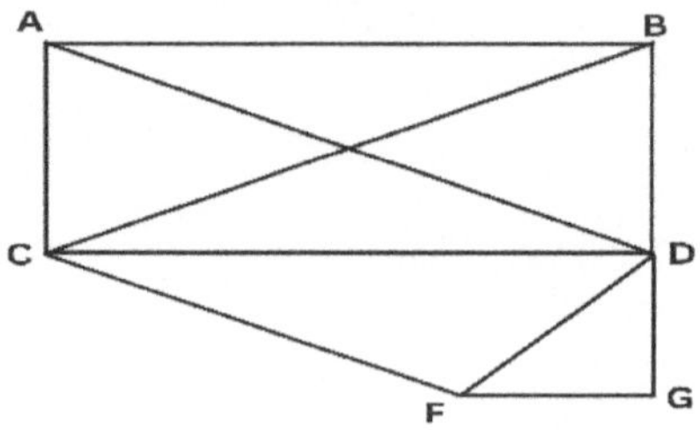

(e) Multiply 10056×2037 using the divide and conquer technique. Apply Karatsuba's method. **4**

(f) Briefly explain any two different approaches to solve the recurrence relation. **5**

2. (a) Arrange the following growth rates in increasing order:
$O(2^n)$, $O(n^3)$, n!, $\sqrt{n}$ **2**

(b)(i) Traverse the following graph using BFS. The starting node is A: **4**

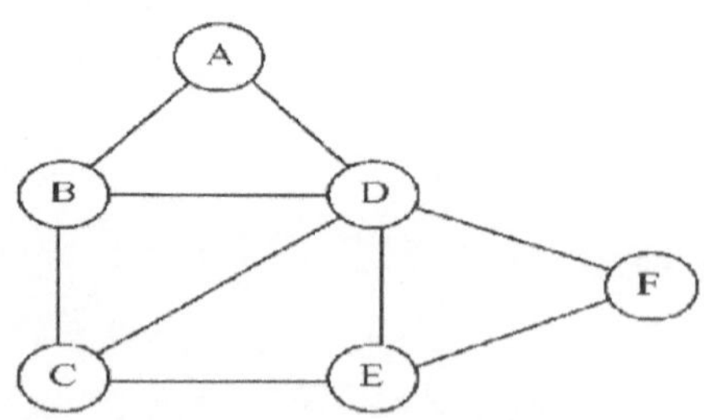

(ii) Perform the complexity analysis of the above algorithm. **4**

3. (a) Explain the basic concept of the quicksort algorithm and apply it to sort the following list of numbers:
15 10 5 4 25 35 7 8
Show all the intermediate steps. **7**

(b) Define the term backtracking and enlist any two problems that can be solved by backtracking. **3**

4. (a) Write a recurrence relation for the following recursive factorial function: **3**

```
int fact(int n)
```

```
{
  if (n == 1)
      return 1;
  else
    return n * fact(n - 1);
}
```

(b) State Horner's rule for polynomial evaluation and apply the rule for evaluating the following polynomial expression:

$$p(x)=6x^7 + 7x^6 - 5x^5 + 3x^3 + 6x^2 + 8x + 7$$

Show stepwise iteration. **7**

5. (a) How many comparisons are needed for the binary search algorithm in a set of 64 elements? **3**

(b) Write Prim's algorithm to solve the minimum cost spanning tree problem and explain. **7**

BCS – 042

Bachelor Of Computer Applications (BCA) (Revised)
Chapter 17: Term-End Examination, June, 2022
BCS-042: Introduction to Algorithm Design

Time: 2 Hours
Maximum Marks: 50

Note: (i) Question No. 1 is compulsory.
(ii) Attempt any three Questions from the rest.

1. (a) Define basic efficiency classes in the context of running time. **3**

(b) Perform linear and binary search to find 15 in the given list of numbers below:
5 7 9 12 13 15 21 25
Count the number of comparisons in both search methods. **6**

(c) Define a recurrence relation. Draw a recurrence tree for the following recurrence relation:
$T(n) = 2T(n/2) + 1$ **5**

(d) Apply Kruskal's algorithm to find the minimum cost spanning tree. **6**

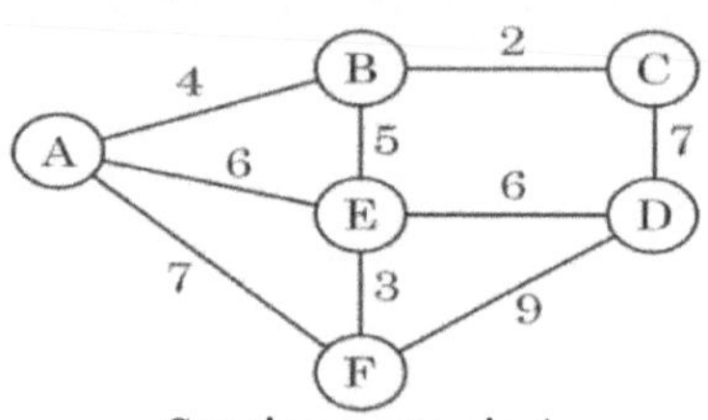

Starting vertex is A.

2. (a) Arrange the following functions in increasing order:
$\log_2^n$, $n \log_2^n$, n^2, $5n+7$ **2**

(b) List any two applications of BFS/DFS. **2**

(c) Write the algorithm for left-to-right binary exponentiation evaluation and apply the algorithm for evaluating a^{280}. Show all the steps. **6**

3. (a) For the function defined by:
$f(n)=6n^2+8n+6$,
show that $f(n)=O(n^2)$ **4**

(b) Show that Dijkstra's algorithm may not work if edges can have negative weight. **3**

(c) Traverse the complete graph on four vertices using BFS and write the sequence of vertices that would be visited by the graph traversal algorithm. **3**

4. (a) Write a recurrence relation for the Fibonacci series problem. **3**

(b) Write and apply the Merge Sort algorithm to sort the following list of integer numbers:
15, 8, 7, 4, 25, 30, 5, 13
Show all the intermediate steps. **7**

5. (a) Write any two cases of the Master method with formal notations. **4**

(b) Write recurrence relations for matrix multiplication using Strassen's method and solve it using the Master method. **6**

BCS – 042

Bachelor Of Computer Applications (BCA) (Revised)
Chapter 18: Term-End Examination, December, 2022
BCS-042: Introduction to Algorithm Design

Time: 2 Hours
Maximum Marks: 50

Note: (i) Question No. 1 is compulsory.
(ii) Attempt any three Questions from the rest.

1. (a) Define Θ (big theta) notation. By using a basic definition, show that $7n^2+8n-9=\Theta(n^2)$ **4**

(b) Apply the Bubble sort algorithm to sort the following list of numbers. Show the procedure step-by-step. Calculate the number of exchange and comparison operations required in the algorithm: **4**

15	8	7	11	25	13	12	4

(c) Solve the following recurrence problem using the recursion tree method: **6**

$$T(n) = 4T(n/2) + n$$

(d) Draw any three spanning trees of the following weighted connected graph: **6**

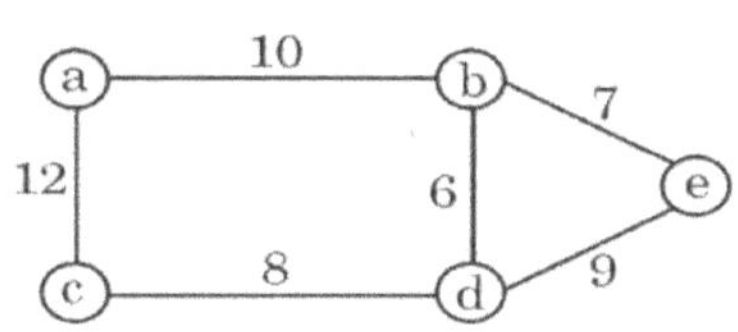

2. (a) Give an example for each complexity class: $O(n)$, $O(n^2)$, $O(n \log n)$ **3**

(b)(i) Write the Euclid algorithm to compute GCD of two non-negative integers and apply it to find GCD (325, 95). Show all the intermediate steps. **4**

(ii) Perform the complexity analysis of the above algorithm. **3**

3. (a) Compare between Kruskal's and Prim's algorithms. **3**

(b) Apply Strassen's algorithm to multiply two matrices A(4x4) and B(4x4) using the divide and conquer technique and explain. **7**

4. (a) Define the term Branch and Bound and write the problem which can be solved through this technique. **3**

(b) Apply Dijkstra's algorithm to find the shortest path from V_1 to all other nodes. Show all the intermediate steps and explain. **7**

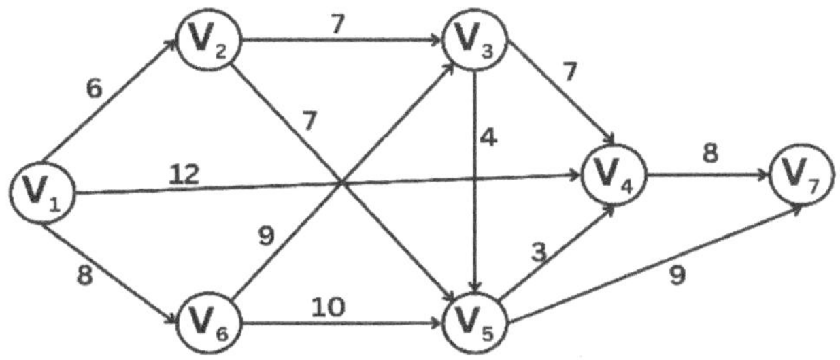

5. (a) Define the terms: path, cycle, and a complete graph. **3**

(b) Write a program to generate the Fibonacci series of 10 terms and count **7**
(i) the number of times the loop will continue, and

(ii) the number of times the assignment operations will occur.

BCS – 042

Bachelor Of Computer Applications (BCA) (Revised)
Chapter 19: Term-End Examination, June, 2023
BCS-042: Introduction to Algorithm Design

Time: 2 Hours
Maximum Marks: 50

Note: (i) Question No. 1 is compulsory.
(ii) Attempt any three Questions from the rest.

1. (a) What is complexity of an algorithm? Explain space complexity and time complexity of algorithms with the help of an example. **5**

(b) Write linear search algorithm and do an analysis of this algorithm for the best case and worst case. **5**

(c) Using the mathematical induction method, show that for all positive integers nnn:

$1^2+2^2+3^2+...+n^2=(n(n+1)(2n+1))/6$

(d) What is Adjacency Matrix? Write the adjacency matrix for the following graph: **5**

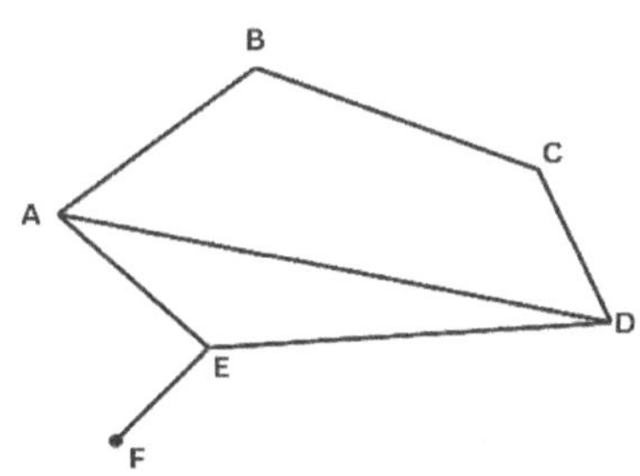

2.(a) Write Depth-First Search (DFS) algorithm. Also, traverse the following graph using DFS from node A. **7**

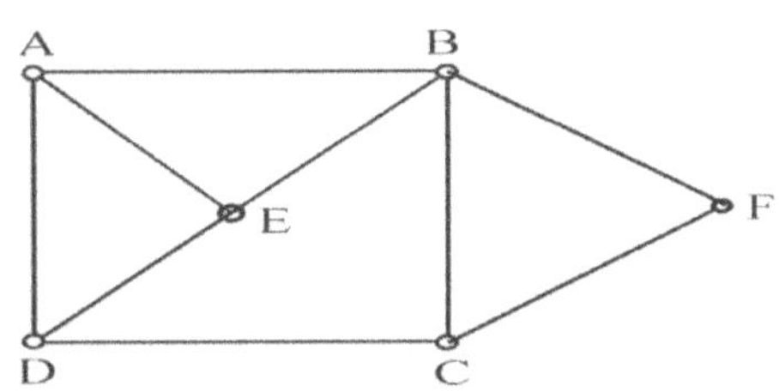

(b) Solve the following recurrence relation using the recurrence tree method:

$T(n)=4T(n/2)+ n$ **3**

3.(a) Write Kruskal's algorithm for finding the Minimum Cost Spanning Tree (MCST). Find MCST of the following graph using Kruskal's algorithm. **8**

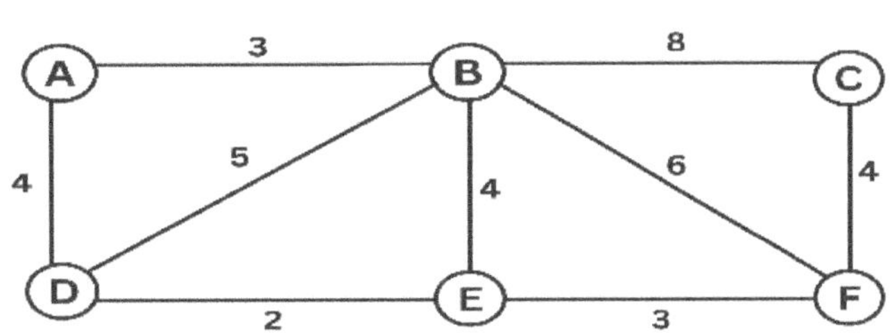

(b) Explain the use of Big O (O) notation in the analysis of algorithms with an example. **2**

4.(a) Find the optimal solution to the knapsack (fractional) problem for n=5 and m=10, where n is the number of objects and m is the capacity of the knapsack. **6**

Profit and Weight of each object are given below:
$(P_1, P_2, P_3, P_4, P_5) = (10, 30, 35, 20, 40)$
$(W_1, W_2, W_3, W_4, W_5) = (3, 5, 2, 6, 11)$

(b) In the context of algorithm study, explain the following with the help of an example of each: **4**
(i) Upper Bound
(ii) Backtracking

5.(a) Sort the following list using the Bubble Sort algorithm. Show the steps of sorting: **6**
30, 8, 7, 14, 20, 28, 10, 6

(b) Write an algorithm for adding two matrices of order m×n and find its time complexity. **4**

BCS – 042

Bachelor Of Computer Applications (BCA) (Revised)
Chapter 20: Term-End Examination, December,2023
BCS-042: Introduction to Algorithm Design

Time: 2 Hours
Maximum Marks: 50

Note: (i) Question No. 1 is compulsory.
(ii) Attempt any three Questions from the rest.

1.(a) Show that: 2

$5n^2+2n + 2 = \Theta(n^2)$

(b) Solve the following recurrence relation: 3

$T(n)=3T(n/2)+n$

(c) Write binary search algorithm and explain its best case and worst case complexity. 5

(d) Represent the following graph using Adjacency List: 4

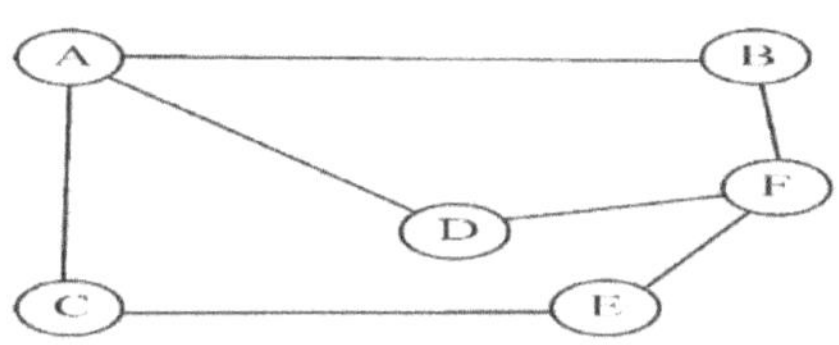

(e) Sort the following list of elements using Quick Sort. Also, show the steps of the operation:

8, 29, 30, 6, 25, 7, 8, 9 6

2.(a) Define the following terms:

(i) Connected graph

(ii) Cycle in an undirected graph 4

(b) Write Euclid's algorithm for finding GCD and explain it. 6

3.(a) What is a spanning tree? Explain the application of spanning trees. 4

(b) Write and explain Dijkstra's single source shortest path algorithm. 6

4.(a) Briefly explain the Greedy technique for designing an algorithm. 4

(b) Write DFS traversal sequence from the node A for the graph: 6

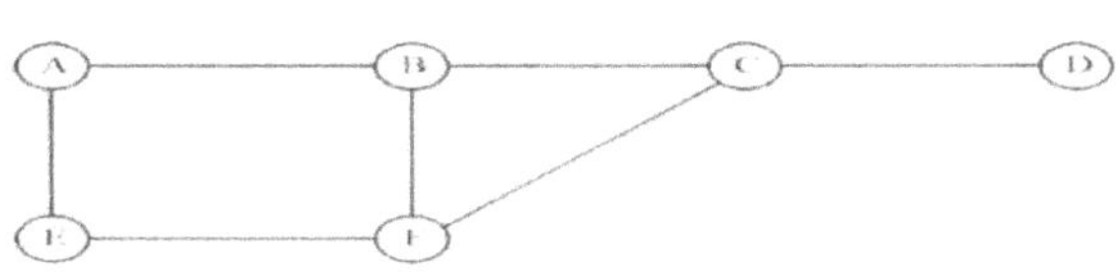

5.(a) Using the mathematical induction method, show that for all positive integers n:

$1+2+3+...+n= (n(n+1))/2$ 5

(b) Write Prim's algorithm for finding the minimum spanning tree and find the complexity of this algorithm. 5

9 789369 721481

Printed at Repro India Ltd.